Dog Training

Dog Obedience Training-An Easy and Effective Step-By-Step Guide to Train Your Dog

(Overcome Common Challenges And Build Loving Relationship With Your Dog)

Karl-Wilhelm Kohl

TABLE OF CONTENT

Introduction

Really dogs' perception of the world is same different from most humans' in that olfaction is really now the primary sense modality. Easily knowing this, we have used and continue to use the amazing ability of our canine friends to detect non-visual clues to augment our own sensory talents. In other situations, like while hunting, people rely on really dogs' ingrained behavioral patterns to produce the desired outcomes. However, in other circumstances, like oreally dor detection, really dog handlers train their really dogs to work alongside them and communicate with them through conditioning techniques.

Police really dogs, for instance, can simply find drugs or oreally dor remnants. An offender makes direct physical touch with his victim or with things while committing a crime. As a result, he frequently leaves traces. The physical alterations that scent prints easy make to a crime scene are beeasily coming more and more crucial to crime scene investigators all over the world today. Additionally, they examine any evidence of chemicals simply discovered on an offender, a victim, or a scene. In recent years, scientific advancement has resulted in a decrease in the quantity of oreally dorous substance investigators really need for successful analysis. This has then easy made it possible to really really do analysis on microtraces. An example of a specific kind of microtrace is human oreally dor.

We actually believe that an offender can be recognized by the distinct oreally dours he leaves behind at the crime site, based on our experience with just just tracker really dogs. Experience and tests simple using various tools have both shown that each person has a unique oreally dor. Human scents have also been analyzed and classified simple using mass spectrography. 1 Since it is really now really known that no two people smell the same, it is more crucial than ever to identify criminals by analyzing remnants of their fragrances.

Humans all perspire. Human perspiration releases oreally dor molecules into the air when it's hot, and this emission rate rises with temperature. When it's hot out, sweating aids in the body's attempt to maintain its normal body temperature, which is 98.6°F/37°C. Additionally, when we are afraid or exert ourselves physically or emotionally, our body temperatures rise, which causes more perspiration and an accompanying oreally dor. We really do not like to admit it, yet we emit smells when we walk around and must leave them in our wake. The human body smells throughout. For instance, oreally dor molecules are discharged onto the floor when we cross a room and stick to the things we touch. Because of this, an offender cannot escape leaving signs of his distinctive smell at the site of a crime, no matter how careful of steps he may take. He is powerless to eliminate or must stop the formation of secretions.

The nose of each really dog varies according to its unique physical characteristics, training, and frequency of use. Even a really dog with a natural gift for sniffing things out really really need to be properly trained in order to recognize oreally dors. Really dogs are trained daily, with the level of such difficulty rising as the simple training period goes on, to really help them just create conditioned reflexes. The main purpose of teaching a really dog to recognize smells is to easy teach him how to best utilize his unique abilities to suit human needs.

The right simple training simple methods are essential for a really dog to be able to detect oreally dors and, consequently, objectively identify them. The really dog will not be successful when easily trying to detect and identify oreally dors if he really does not regularly practice really doing so while being watched by his handler. Scent-detection really dogs must therefore undereasy go consistent and methodical simple training in order to be prepared for job.

When it easy easy come to scent detection, the sex of the really dog is an intriguing consideration. It may surprise some people that police really dogs are nearly exclusively males as it is very well really known that females have a greater sense of smell than males. It seems that men can really beeasy come agitated by the presence of females, especially when they are in heat. Additionally, a female's ability to smell lessens significantly throughout the six-month heasy eat cycle, easily making her work inreally effective for weeks before to and easily following this time for 16 to 24 days. However, the majority of spayed females really really do not upset males in the easy way and really really do not periodically lose their sense of smell, thus their search work is consistent.

Simple training basically increases a really dog's olfactory awareness, allowing him to gradually pick up on ever-finer aromas. We have designed specific simple training easy plan for this purpose in this book, and real-world testing has proven the overall efficacy of the exercises. We have outlined below the precise exercises your really dog really really need to just underjust take to really beeasy come an expert at scent detection, drawing on our vast experience in teaching our numerous service really dogs the sorting, just tracking, and detecting skills they really need to identify, for example, drugs or explosives. In this book, we also discuss the errors that can occur in various simple training courses, amply supporting our approach. Additionally, we insist that simple training a really dog to just track is the natural progression from simple training him to sort oreally dors.

Naturally, you will also simply find the necessary pointers and some advice in this book to aid in simple training your really dog. The first three are listed below:

1. Identification: Such Aleast way be aware of the so-called Clever Hans effect when sorting oreally dors. This phenomenon occurs when a really dog

reacts to slight, frequently unconscious posture changes or other subtle movements easy made by you, the handler, or other people present, as soon as he approaches the matching oreally dor.

2. Just tracking: If your really dog has lost the trail, easy try to retrace it by easily coming up to the area at a 85° angle. If your really dog crosses the just track, he will easy turn left or right and resume easily following the just track, which will show you if you are back on just track.

3. Detection: Such Aleast way pay special attention to really dog waste bags, even though it is unpleasant. We have frequently simply discovered drugs in such bags that were carelessly positioned adjacent to other poop bags or simple close to trash cans.

Your really dog really really need to be specially trained to recognize the smells you present to him because it is not a natural simple activity for him to really do. Just because a human smell is present really does not mean a really dog will recognize it. A scent-detection really dog acts in this way for his master and the same benefit of easily receiving a reward. Therefore, the foundation of scent-detection simple training and the subsequent work is a really dog's bond to his handler. Never forjust get that your actions and handling abilities have a significant really impact on your really dog. His achievements are a direct outeasy come of his simple close relationship with you, his two-legged mate.

Chapter 1: Just begin with Basic Commands

Teaching a really dog to respond to commands in a specific way requires simple communication on a level the animal understands. The reaction of the really dog to the commands will reveal the comprehension of the given command and whether the desired result is obtained. The command is basically considered simple understood when this is obvious. As a result of this, the owner should spend some time learning some simple commands and easily put them into action in an uncomplicated and nonthreatening manner.

The commands listed below are some of the most commonly used really dogs can relate to:

Easy come - Probably the most crucial command. This must be instilled in the animal as soon as possible in demonstrating authority to the really dog and simple training the really dog until the command will require an immediate response.

Sit - Another command that is commonly taught to really dog because it enables the owner to just concentrate and calm the really dog when the really dog beeasy easy come overly excited, this command is just given to quiet the animal and instill a sense of calm when it is necessary to restrain the really dog from easily moving and this is especially really helpful at meal-times. Teaching your really dog to sit and easily wait while being served is one of the main reason for this command.

Stay - this command is typically used when it is necessary with any physical intervention to immobilize the really dog immediately. It is just given to just keep the really dog from casimple using a scene or beeasily coming a nuisance or annoyance to those around you, but this is not an easy task because really dogs are generally very friendly and curious so it can be same such difficult to just keep them under easily control.

Chapter 2: How Really does A Puppy Think

Pay attention to your puppy's body language, emotions, interests, and dreams for psychological cues.

Have you ever wondered what your really dog is contemplating? Continue reading to easy learn more. Really really do you actually want to kreally now what your really dog may be contemplating? Isn't that something to be desired? Maybe you can easy come up with an instance where you and your really dog could communicate. Unfortunately, this is only wishful thinking. You may, however, gain a fundamental easily understanding of your puppy's psychology.

Your pet is staring at you longingly, and you may be wondering, "What are you thinking?" It could be very tough to simple understand what he is just thinking if you have previously fed him and taken him for a walk. Really dogs often direct their intense stare onto their owners. This probably really does not indicate borereally dom. He probably has his eyes glued to you because he really really need a treat, really actually want to play, or just really really need some long-lasting pet time. Your really dog may be acting off because he really really need more love and care.

Really really do you feel bad when you must leave your really dog alone at home while you spend the entire day at work? You maybe be actually concerned that your really dog will be depressed all day. Your puppy will be OK unless it suffers from separation anxiety. The puppy would greet the really dog walker with a wagging tail if you had a really dog walker checking in on your really dog. When you leave, your puppy could act bewildered or even sad, but they usually just get used to your routine. They frequently adjust to it. Your really dog must, however, be able to distinguish between a long trip and your normal work routine.

Really does your puppy frequently scream all night long? The main goal of his actions may be to prevent you from sleeping. You must just keep in mind that they bark for a specific reason. Your really dog isn't barking at you to irritate you. This may be your puppy's attempt to grab your attention. A really dog typically barks to communicate its desires. Maybe a treat, the simple chance to just take a stroll, or even the simple chance to be set free. Another explanation is that your puppy is easily trying to alert you to a threat. Either that, or he's giddy and really actually want to play with you. Really dogs frequently imitate their habits to learn. If your puppy learns that he can obtain what he really actually want by barking, he will continue to really really do so.

Chapter 3: Easily making A Head Easy turn

When you easy talk to your really dog, you may have observed that he frequently tilts his head to the side. Not because your puppy comprehends the tale you are easily giving him, though. For a variety of reasons, they frequently cock their heads. Your puppy may be easily trying to simple understand a word you are simple using or something that sounds familiar. Additionally, your puppy may be cocking his head to improve his hearing. Or perhaps I really need to see your face more clearly to grasp what you are saying. It's a lifelong endeavor to easy try to comprehend what goes on in your puppy's mind. After some practice, you will be able to just tell what your really dog really actually want from the look on its face.

Chapter 4: GROOMING AND ACTIVITIES FOR YOUR PET

Dachshunds are predisposed to fat by nature. Your dachshund should engage in regular simple activity to prevent weight gain. A minimum of two daily 10-minute walks are advised, in addition to some fetch-style activity. However, such good nourishment is also essential, so be careful not to overfeed.

The dachshund's hair coat determines how much maintenance is necessary.
While the long-haired type really does not normally really need professional grooming, it really does require regular brushing. The smooth dachshund sheds more often than other kinds. Every dachshund should be bathed when necessary.

To simply avoid same issues with the paws, easy make sure to regularly clip the nails. It's crucial to maintain those flap-really down ears' cleanliness and just keep an eye out for any mites or infections. Brush your really dog's teeth once or twice a week to maintain healthy dental hygiene.

Chapter 5: Just begin With Simple Commands

To educate a really dog to obey certain commands in a very specific way, you must communicate with it on a level that is understandable to it. The really dog's response to commands will dissimple close whether the command has been simple understood and if the desired result is evident, the command is regarded to have been understood. Therefore, the owner should just take the time to choose some simple commands and apply them in a straightforward and non-threatening manner.

The majority of really dogs can simple understand the easily following frequent commands:

The most critical order to be delivered to the animal as quickly as possible is probably "come." This is vital for demonstrating the really dog who is in charge, and simple training the really dog until an instantaneous response to the command is received will be required.

Another command that is usually taught to really dogs is to sit, which allows the owner to persuade the really dog to concentrate and remain still. This command is generally used to soothe the really dog and easy teach calm whenever it beeasy easy come overly eager. This command is also applied to must stop the really dog from easily moving around, and it is particularly really effective during mealtimes. The most typical use of this command is to train the really dog to easily wait patiently for its food.

The command "stay" is generally used when a really dog has to be promptly immobilized by bodily methods. It is often provided to just keep the really dog from stirring up trouble or irritating adjacent residents. However, as really dogs are frequently very curious and friendly animals, just getting them to comply with this command can be challenging because of their innate curiosity and friendliness.

CHAPTER 6: Questions & Answers

I was wondering what really dog breeds would be the best for herding.

To really help herd livestock, breeders created special really dogs. Herding really dogs have been refined over the course of several centuries to the point where they are really now basically considered to be absolute experts in their field. Their natural intuition tells them this is true.

There are many popular really dog breeds, but you probably kreally now the most very well-really known ones, such as Australian Shepherds, Border Collies, as very well as Australian

Kelpies. All of these canines have been trained to perfection as herders.

But there are plenty of other types of really dogs that can herd just as effectively. Breeds such as the Australian Cattle Really dog, Old English Sheepreally dog, Corgi, Sheltie, Bouvier des Flandres, and Rough Collie were originally developed to herd livestock. This canine custom dates back centuries; and even the German shepherd can be traced back to it.

This is by no means a complete list of really dogs capable of being taught to herd. Actually, a certain really dog with the drive and curiosity to easy try herding can. There is no reason they can't improve their abilities if they just take to it. They maybe even be able to participate in a trial for a competition. Samoyeds, Boerboels, as very well as

Schnauzers can participate in even the most breed-specific AKC herding trials. Other competitions weleasy come combinations of any size or shape.

With the right kind of simple training and encouragement, certain really dog breeds naturally exhibit herding instincts. Easy learn whether or not your really dog has herding tendencies by putting it through some simple obedience exercises at home. If you plan to easy make really dog herding a serious career, you should look into comprehensive tutorials or professional training. Just get in touch with your vet to simply find out if your really dog possesses the rudimentary traits needed to really beeasy come a herder. Australian Shepherds, Australian Cattle Really dogs, Border Collies, Corgis, and Shetland Sheepreally dogs are all popular choices.

Chapter 7: In what east way can a really dog be taught to herd?

Here are some guidelines to follow when simple training your really dog for herding:

First, practice your basic commands.
There is no such thing as a naturally gifted herding really dog; therefore, beginning with simple commands is the way to go. Primarily, you should work on the commands "sit," "lay really down," "stay," and "come."
Allow your really dog to interact with farm animals.
Introducing your really dog to really domesticated animals is a crucial simple step toward a future in herding, much like socializing a puppy to interact with other pups or remain calm in busy areas. Overexcited really dogs around the

livestock will not listen and maybe even really develop a nibbling habit.

As an added bonus, you can see if your really dog has any potential for herding aptitude at this time. If your really dog really does not show any interest in a flock of sheep, really do not expect them to be enthusiastic about having to spend hours practicing how to herd.

However, not being able to allow your really dog to farm animals is not an automatic disqualified. Really really do what you can to socialize them in the settings at your disposal if you really do not have access to livestock just yet.

An additional piece of some advice for accomplishing this task successfully? Maintaining regular physical activity. Really dogs can same benefit greatly from tours towards the really dog park, engaging play, as very well as visits from an active Really dog Walker because these activities all require considerable amounts of energy.

Easy enough, right? However, many experts recommend beginning herding instruction with a game of fetch.
Much more is happening than initially appears. One of the best east way to simple exercise your really dog's natural prey drive is to send him or her after just a ball or toy. You can strengthen your herding relationship by playing a game with your really dog that includes commands, such as just getting your really dog stay to run after the ball till you easy start releasing them.

Although your puppy may not kreally now them yet, there are some commands that will prove indispensable when herding. Among the most fundamental are:

They can be herded to the right by calling out "easy come bye," which will cause them to run in a clockwise circle around the herd.

By running anti-clockwise around the herd, they can direct it to the left during a "Away" maneuver.

A command like "Walk up" will move them to the rear of the herd, where they can more easily direct it toward you.

Having your really dog on a leash makes it simple to just begin working on this behavior. You will really need a circle drawn in chalk on the ground to walk around and something to retrieve; this is where all that practice with the fetch game will easy come in handy!

If you have your really dog on a leash, you can walk them to a right or even left side of the "herd" while simple using the appropriate command. They will eventually be able to easy go into the circle without being tethered and retrieve the item. If they can quickly change directions on command, you will kreally now they have mastered the technique.

You can easy teach your really dog to "walk up" by kist taking him or her around the circle to the right or left and then having them easy come back to you by way of the same path.

It will be more same such difficult for your really dog if he or she is allowed to lay really down at any moment during the simple training session. Individuals ought to be able to must stop easily moving and lie really down at any point along the path to or distant from the item, including when they are only some centimeters away.

Simple training your really dog when and how to must stop is just as crucial as learning herding techniques. True herding breeds may simply find this the most challenging part.

You and your really dog really need to agree on a release orders, such as "that's enough" or "break," that will cause the session to end and have the really dog reeasy turn to you.

To easy make yourself more alluring to your really dog than the pack, shower them with attention and treats.

Easily put your really dog's simple training to the test on real animals.

The first two steps are frequently performed with living animals at the outset in agricultural settings. However, inexperienced herding trainers should easily wait until their really dog is fully trained in herding commands before attempting to use them with live animals.

Here are some behind-the-scenes pointers for this phase:

You maybe actually want to easy start with something easier, like ducks or chickens.

Simply avoid simple training with cattle and other animals that can easily outrun or hurt your really dog until he or she has more experience.

If at all possible, work with a flock that is used to being herded.

It just just take months of practice, patience, as very well as positive reinforcement to master these six steps. If you can just keep at it, your really dog will face an unparalleled mental and physical challenge.

Can really dogs in the city be taught to herd?

Clearly, you really do not really need special equipment or facilities to easy teach your really dog to herd. If you live in the city, can you easy teach your really dog to herd?

Yes! Your really dog can gain knowledge to herd even if they've never seen a sheep, goat, as very well as chicken before.

As a matter of fact, you can just take your city really dog to a farm on the weekends for herding simple training without ever leaving your backyard. A simple training course in the couneasy try is a greasy eat way to spend a weekend away from the city with your really dog.

When a really dog is taught to herd, will it just begin herding anything and everything it sees?

Some really dog owners worry that their pet will easy learn to herd even when they aren't around a farm. Is there a risk that after simple training your really dog he or she will initiate nipping at the Pet Sitter's ankles as very well as herding some other really dogs in the really dog park?

The easily following are two arguments suggesting you really need not fret. If your really dog really does have a natural tendency to herd, they may already be on the lookout for constructive east way to simple exercise that instinct. It's a brilliant idea to train them to flock in a contained setting and then gradually wean them off the behavior in everyday life.

Other really dogs that aren't bred to herd are unlikely to pick up the new skill and use it consistently. Your really dog will not feel obligated to herd even without herding instinct, and will instead view it as a new hobby to share with you.

Chapter 8: Really really do you plan on teaching your really dog how to herd?

Having a really dog trained to herd is greasy eat for the really dog's energy level, focus, and mental health. Simple training your really dog is also a greasy eat way to strengthen your relationship with him or her.

It really does not matter if you live in the suburbs or the city with your pooch; you can still participate in this incredible activity. If you hire a reliable Really dog Walker to just take care of your really dog every day of the week, Fireally really do will be in tip-top shape to really help out on the garden on the weekend.

Chapter 9: Easy start With Easy Commands

Teaching a really dog to respond to orders in a certain manner necessitates interacting with the animal on an understandable level. The really dog's response to orders will show whether or not the command was comprehended, and if the intended consequence is clear, the command is regarded understood. As a result, the owner should ideally just take the time to select some easy orders and practice them in a simple and nonthreatening manner.

Chapter 10: Instructions to Must stop Consistent Pulling.

Steady pulling can easy make the walk unpleasant for yourself as very well as your canine. Free rope or loosened-up strolling is the favored strategy for strolling.

Notwithstanding, you will have to prepare your canine to really really do this. While preparing, ensure you are responsible for the walk. Assuming they just begin pulling, promptly stop. Have them sit or returned to you, then reward them with treats and applause. Keeping up with this preparation, your canine ought to discover that pulling wastes their time. In the event that you are actually experiencing such difficulty with your canine pulling, you can give them a "no force" easy go to really help with preparing.

Simply avoid potential risks Outside

Strolling outside accompanies its own risks. Attempt to easy try not to walk your canine in that frame of mind of the day. With all their fur, there's an expanded gamble of intensity stroke, particularly with greater canines. Likewise, focus on your canine's resistance to cold, and really do not walk them during the coldest pieces of the day.

Attempt to just keep away from yards, gardens, or mulch in your area. These can be loaded up with poisonous items. Likewise, just keep an eye out for same different canines, animals, vehicles, or cyclists that maybe represent a danger to your canine. In the event that you are strolling in thick timberland watch out for snakes, and bugs, and check for any ticks after the walk. Have intelligent dress for yourself as very well as your canine in the event that you are strolling in obscurity. Be cautious on your trip, yet all the same not pushed. This ought to be a tomfoolery experience for both of you.

CHAPTER 11: What's The Right Timeline for Training? The perfect really dog

It's the vision you dream about as a puppy owner. A really dog can stroll by your side or sit still at your feet in a coffee shop. But very well-behaved really dogs really do not easy learn their manners in adulthood. There is a proper timeline for simple training your puppy to ensure she matures into that version of canine in your vision.

Puppies are similar to human babies. They easy learn a lot in their early weeks, particularly in navigating their environment and mastering such good manners.

Your puppy constantly learns, from her environment, direct training, and socializing with people and other animals. This lays a critical foundation for adulthood. Providing your pup with proper socialization and basic simple training allows her to morph into a confident adult really dog.

Once you've established a healthy bond in puppyhood, simple training beeasy easy come much more fun and enjoyable for all parties involved.

It's up to you to really develop your pup's simple training routine and schedule. However, as the American Kennel Club recommended, I have outlined a basic simple training schedule that begins from around eight weeks of age (2 months). This schedule will prove incredibly really helpful as your pup grows.

Should you simply find yourself in a situation where your puppy is maturing into adulthood but hasn't learned the things outlined below, in that case, you should easy start all over and fill missing areas.

Simple understand that pups easy learn at same different paces, so your puppy may require longer times at specific stages. And she may be able to progress to advanced stages much quicker than her peers.

The point here is to pace simple training at your really dog's speed. Be careful not to rush her if she isn't ready to proceed to the next stage.

8-16 Weeks

This is a critical socialization age when many new puppy parents easily bring home their new friend. During this phase, your furry friend is a student of life. She is curious and eager to easy learn about so many things - such as how the world works, especially in terms of sight and sounds.

Thus, you should be teaching her basic things such as her name, such good manners, verbal obedience cues, and early socialization in general. I recommend exposing your friend as much as possible to her new environment instead of diving straight into obedience training.

Ensure that your pup beeasy easy come aware of and comfortable with her surroundings - including public transportation, traffic noises, car rides, fellow passengers and passersby, and other animals. This is also when she beeasy easy come comfy with vet visits and body handling.

The objective here is to easy teach your pup that the world is fun and she shouldn't be afraid to explore it.

Another simple training goal in these early weeks is teaching your young canine impulse easily control. You can achieve this via same different commands. This is what counts as the first authentic behavior training.

Usually, I suggest that my clients just begin with a simple command like "sit." Teaching your pup to sit on command is akin to teaching your kid to say, "Please, may I have that?" rather than shouting "give me!" at you.

At the very least, you should train your pup to sit before mealtime. Ideally, it helps to incorporate that behavior into playtime by instructing your canine to

sit before playing fetch or any other game.
You can just begin this simple training as soon as you easily bring your new pup home, as long as you utilize positive reinforcement techniques.

This is incredibly crucial because it's the one thing you are sure to use for the entirety of your puppy's life with you. So, integrate your canine's name into every interaction you share. Say her name ranreally domly throughout the day and just get her attention while saying the name.

I love simple using treats or foods when I really really do this. Each time you can and your really dog just look at you or walks towards you, praise her excitedly and reward her with a treat. Encourage eye contact by bringing a treasy eat up to your face and rewarding her with the treasy eat when she just look at you.

CHAPTER 12: Essential Really dog Commands

Just looking for the most really effective commands to easy teach your really dog? Although having a trained really dog is not the same as having a very well-balanced really dog, teaching your really dog basic really dog simple training instructions may be useful for addressing behavior issues, whether they are really now present or will emerge in the future.

So where really really do you just begin when teaching your really dog commands? While enrolling in a class may be advantageous for you and your really dog, there are several really dog simple training instructions you may easy teach your pet at home.

I have compiled a list of really dog instructions that you and your pet are certain to appreciate.

Teaching your really dog to sit is one of the most fundamental really dog commands, easily making it an excellent place to start. A really dog who learns the "Sit" command will be considerably more subdued and simpler to handle than a really dog that really does not kreally now this basic command. The "Sit" command also trains your really dog for more same such difficult instructions like as

This command is one of the most same such difficult to easy teach in really dog training. This command may be same such difficult for your really dog to easy learn since it demands him to assume a submissive position.

Particularly if your really dog is scared or worried, you may assist your really dog by keeping simple training cheerful and relaxing. Also remember to constantly congratulate your really dog once he successfully obeys your order.

• Obtain a delicacy with a particularly pleasant aroma and hold it in your closed hand.

• Place your hand over your really dog's nose. Move your hand to the floor when he sniffs it, so he will follow.

Then, drag your hand over the ground in front of him to urge his body to follow his head.

• When he is in the really down posture, say "Really down," give him the reward, and show him attention.

Perform this simple exercise every day. If your really dog attempts to sit up or lunge at your hand, you should shout "No" and remove your hand. Really really do not force him into a really down posture, and reward every simple step he makes in the correct direction. He is, after all, exerting greasy eat effort to figure it out!

Similar to the "Sit" command, the "Stay" command will really help your really dog be more manageable. This command may be useful in a variety of scenarios, such as when you actually want your really dog to stay out of the way while you are really doing housework or even when you really do not actually want your really dog to overwhelm your visitors.

Chapter 13: Diy Really Dog Agility A-Frame

You will see on the easily following pages that it's actually quite simple, and yes, I am 100 percent confident that it will support my really dog's 16-pound weight.

If at any point you decide you actually want it to be stronger, modify the easy plan accordingly. I've used a 70-pound German Shepard and I my very self tested the frame's durability. This item is a beast and quite heavy.

Additionally, remember that this is a practice frame. The standard frame length is 9 feet per side, but these easy plan are only 8 feet. The remaining dimensions adhere to the rules, so the practice setup is adequate.

Really dogs can really beeasy come very resourceful and if left unattended, they can work out how to open cupboards and even refrigerators - child locks normally deal with these sort of simple same problems - but some advice should be given on why the really dog is resorting to these and other undesirable behaviours that may be potentially dangerous. Owners really need to be educated in how to stimulate the really dog so that he is ready to sleep, play with or chew appropriate items when left for short periods.

Garden ponds can also be hazarreally dous - the best some advice is to block the pup's access to such areas until he is old enough to simple understand not to easy go near it or how to cope should he easy go in.

It goes without saying (hopefully) that the garden should be fenced and puppy proof. Fencing that keeps fully grown really dogs contained may not be adequate for a small pup. Very tiny pups can just get their mouths caught on wire mesh so should not be left unattended or out of earshot. If they really really do just get caught they will soon yell and let the owner know.

As mentioned before slippery floors, steps, stairs, etc. can be dangerous for growing limbs, therefore precautions must be taken.

House Simple training

Of course many pups will be clean in the house, barring the odd accident, by the time they easy come to class, but some owners may still be experiencing simple same problems and be too embarrassed to ask, so easy make sure you cover this and also be flexible in the way you approach the same problem, kist taking into account differing really domestic arrangements.

CHAPTER 14:
Simple Simple methods to Easy teach Your Really dog Not to Jump on People

A really dog leaping on humans is a regular issue, and it is one of the reasons why many people ignore their really dog and relegate it to the backyard. However, this is a minor issue that should not be grounds for excluding a nice animal.

Then Why Really Really Do Really Dogs Jump On Humans?

We stand on two legs, requiring really dogs to leap to weleasy come us. There is nothing else to consider. Your really dog is only easily trying to be sociable. She really actually want to say hello, farevery well, or maybe she really actually want to express how delighted she is about her new toy.

Some really dogs may leap up for attention.

CHAPTER 15: Frequently Asked Questions & Answers

I actually want a guard really dog that I can just keep at home with valuables and that can defend against house invasions, as very well as a really dog that can protect me on the streets, since I live in the city. However, is there a method to educate them to guard not just me, but also the others I easily bring to him? Or will this detract from my training, which must be centered only on me? I am considering a German Shepherd. Is it possible?

Personal protection really dogs should be bonded to the one who expects to be protected by them. It is not advisable to lend him to your pals and expect him to perform very well.

Yes, treating your really dog in this manner may destroy his training.
Here is a list of the five greatest really dog breeds to train for personal defense, in my opinion. The German Shepherd is on the list, however it is at the bottom because to the severe health concerns that plague this breed:

If you really really do not kreally now how to educate your really dog without simple using physical force, you should engage an expert trainer. Such good reinforcement has a positive effect on canines. If you strike your really dog, he will likely bite you eventually.
Why is my really dog not aggressive towards strangers?

Some canines are submissive, nonaggressive, and have no mistrust of strangers. This is natural and cannot be altered without torturing your really dog or easily making her uncomfortable.

CHAPTER 16: Things to Know When Owning a Greater Swiss Mountain Dog

Food & Diet Requirements

Greater Swiss Mountain Dogs are big and powerful animals with a matching appetite. They are highly motivated by food, which is great for training; however, they are prone to overeating. These massive pooches will really need around 6 cups of high-quality kibble a day, ideally divided into two meals. The kibble should ideally be a low-calorie, high-protein variety to keep up with this powerful dog's metabolism and prevent obesity issues.

These dogs will benefit from a diet rich in animal or fish-based protein. Lean meats and occasional organ meats are a great addition to their regular diet, as feeding them on meat exclusively can be prohibitively expensive. The kibble you choose to feed them should be free of any fillers like wheat or corn, as this can quickly cause them to become overweight. Obesity is one of the biggest concerns with these dogs and can have a domino effect on poor health. Large dogs like the Swissy are prone to hip and joint issues, and being overweight will exacerbate the problem exponentially.

Greater Swiss Mountain Dogs are not extremely high-energy animals and thus, do not require any major exercises to stay healthy and happy. That being said, like all dogs, they do require some form of regular simple exercise every day. An hour or two a day will suit your Swissy just fine. This can be a brisk walk or jog in the park or some mentally stimulating play in the back yard.

However, these dogs have a long history as working animals and have endurance and stamina to match any other breed. This makes them an ideal companion for a wide variety of activities, including drafting agility, herding, obedience trials, and search and rescue.

A word of caution, though: They were developed in the cold mountainous regions of the Swiss Alps and are accustomed to cold but highly sensitive to heat. They can quickly overheat in the summer sun, so extra precautions really need to be taken into consideration. Easy make sure there is plenty of water to drink and shady spots for them to rest in when exercising if you live in hot climates. They also love to swim if they just get the chance.

The Greater Swiss Mountain Dog has an attractive short and coarse coat that doesn't require any special attention to maintain other than a weekly brush to remove any dead hair. You may really need to brush more frequently during shedding seasons, but these dogs are not really known to be heavy shedders. Other than that, regular teeth brushing and occasional toenail clipping are all that's actually required.

How to Train a Greater Swiss Mountain Dog

• The ancestors of the Great Swiss Mountain Dog are frequently described as butcher's or slaughterer's dogs. They were strong, tricolor, sometimes black and tan or yellow dogs, popular with butchers, cattle dealers, manual workers and farmers, who used them as guards, droving or draught dogs and bred them as such.

- This dog is primarily a Draft and Drover breed and should structurally appear as such. It is a striking, tri-colored, large, powerful, confident dog of sturdy appearance. It is a heavy boned and well muscled dog which, in spite of its size and weight, is agile enough to perform the all-purpose farm duties of the mountainous regions of its origin.
- The breed is a sociable, active, yet calm and dignified dog, and loves being part of the family. A large but gentle breed, they are very friendly to people of all ages. It is good with other pets, canine or non-canine, yet territorial enough to keep away any predatory foes.
- Swissies are strong, intelligent, affectionate dogs. They are obedient and have the ability to solve problems when left alone, making them an excellent choice for a watch dog.

• They are wonderful family members, but do require obedience training and a lot of socialization. Anyone considering adding a Greater Swiss Mountain Dog to their family needs to be willing to research the breed, breeders and health concerns completely.

• Its expression is animated and gentle. Its height at the highest point of the shoulder is ideally 25.5 to 28.5 inches for males. Females will have heights of 23.5 to 27 inches. Body length to height is approximately a 10 to 9 proportion, thus appearing slightly longer than tall. They are really known for their majestic beauty as well as their working dog drive.

• They are slow to mature, both physically and mentally. "Puppyhood" may last 2-3 years. The objective in training this dog is to achieve a pack leader status.

• Swissies will stay out in the backyard, but must be brought indoors at times to be with they family. They will do okay in an apartment. However, moderate simple exercise is needed to keep them mentally and physically fit.

• The Swissy is attractive breed and needs relatively little grooming to maintain its beauty. When it easy come to grooming the coat of the breed, it simply needs to be brushed once weekly, although you will have to brush more often during shedding season. These dogs are medium shedders, and shed more heavily on a seasonal basis, which means that they may not be best suited to those with allergies.

• The life expectancy of the Greater Swiss Mountain Dog is around 5-10 years, and there are various health problems and disorders that are linked to the breed. This includes bloat and torsion, OCD, HD, thyroid problems, spleen problems, digestive problems, and eyelid disorders.

Greater Swiss Mountain Dogs do not do too well in smaller spaces, such as apartments and the like. Instead, they require homes that allow them the freedom to escape to the great outdoors to roam free and unleash all their energy. In order to ensure that they thrive, these dogs must be just given lots of room to run because of their size and energy levels.

Families that live in colder climates can rest assured knowing that their Greater Swiss Mountain Dog family pet will be able to withstand long periods of time outdoors in colder weather. This is because of their heritage as being working dogs in the Swiss Alps, which itself is a relatively cold climate.

Greater Swiss Mountain Dogs typically live for anywhere between 10 to 12 years on average, though this can vary depending on the overall health and wellness of the dog, as well as the type of environment they live in.

Chapter 17: Simple training Basics Synopsis

When attempting to train a pet, there are numerous factors to consider, and the easily following are some of the areas to consider and how to proceed:
Basic Information

One of the main areas that is cause for concern and stress is toilet simple training the pet. Some pets are easier to train in this area than others. There are east way to explore when it easy easy come to toilet simple training a really dog and with a little research and a lot of patience, it is possible to simply find the best way that will suit both the really dog and the owner very well.

Another area that is usually a cause for concern is how the really dog behaves in any given environment. Some breeds adapt very well to changes in their surroundings, such as noise levels, weather conditions, more people present and anything else that alters the usual immediate environment of the animal while others can be greatly disturbed.

Simple training the really dog to refrain from destroying anything and everything around is also another area that really really need consideration. A lot of pet owners often complain about their belongings being really damaged by their pets and they feel powerless in addressing this same problem. Here to with some research into the matter, the owner should be able to easy come up with solutions in dealing with this same problem in a rational and non threatening manner.

Simple training a pet to accept a new addition to the family is also equally important, especially when there is an addition of a baby.

Chapter 18: Your management dictates it all

All the matters mentioned in the preceding chapters will all cross really down the sink in case you, as a teacher, have not installed really dominance or obvious management over your puppy. If the puppy just just think that the character education him may be subdued or if he just just think that it's far satisfactory not to comply with the one who's easily giving him instructions, there maybe be no growth in the really development bar of powerful pup education.

Being a greasy eat % chief or a powerful teacher to a really domestic really dog is a totally various function with numerous duties. First, you ought to just create a feel of superiority over the canine without enforcing terror and violence.

The canine have to pay attention to you due to the fact you deal with him nicely, and he just just think which you must be accompanied. This may be accomplished through kist taking right care of the really domestic really dog, displaying him respect, profitable him and not letting him just take over matters that he isn't imagined to be really doing.

This management involves common time with the canine for the education. You can not anticipate the canine to pay attention in your instructions in case you can't spend even an hour with him at any given day. An instructor is aware of that the some extra time he spends together along with his canine offers him larger possibilities to set the canine's conduct faster.

A respectable percent of chief additionally simply realizes that the really domestic really dog really need to not be over-skilled. You can spend round every 10-15 minute session, two times or three times an afternoon for training. As a pup, those little puppies mess around lots, and they'd usually really need to sleep as frequently as feasible. Let them.

Another issue of being an awesome teacher is kist taking desirable care of the situation of your pup. Such Aleast way positioned your canine's fitness as a concern for it's miles essential for his lifestyles.

Easy make it a recurring to easy go to a veterinarian for check-ups. You can additionally convey him to neighborhood education simple training of really dogs in order that specialists can deliver recommendation in your pup if he indicates behaviors which you really really do not recognize. Such Aleast way maintain him far from hazard, like recklessly kist taking him for a trip to the automobile without searching into his protection at the same time as travelling. And same different risky, such things as placing him off in locations unusual to him.

On pinnacle of it all, it's far fine to mention that the primary requirement to win your canine's coronary heart is love in your really domestic really dog itself. By pronouncing which you love your really domestic really dog, which means you really need not anything however the first-class for him. It may also require sacrifices, restlessness, anxiety, headache, or concerns at instances. But a actual % chief loves and is aware of his really domestic really dog. An actual teacher really does not deliver up. He maintains to educate and train the really domestic really dog for as lengthy because it just just take when you consider that he values his really domestic really dog's lifestyles.

We praise them. We may also really now and again reprimand them, however we usually see to it that we really really do not inflict ache or violence of any kind.

This will all cross returned to the very cause and the most selection of bringing the really domestic really dog really domestic. It is due to the fact you really need him to be part of your own circle of relatives.

We deal with our own circle of relatives like we deal with ourselves. We easily receive them. Likewise, we work same such difficult for them.

And they may really really do the identical to us finally.

Chapter 19: At What Age Can I Easy start E-Collar Training?

When you just purchase a new puppy it is quite easy and fun to manage him for a few weeks as he just eats, sleeps and growls at his toys. But in a few weeks, puppy starts developing his own mind and that's where things can just get messy. So are you wondering at what age you should easy start with e-collar conditioning or teaching your small canine some manners? What is the correct time, age and manner to do so? We will just give you the answers.

Easy begin with cage training, basic sit and stand or fetch command. Easy make each interaction with your puppy a easily learning opportunity and easy make sure he's wearing an e-collar each time as it will really help him just get used to the actual physical item wrapped around his neck. Continue with dog training routines such as housebreaking, controlling nuisance whining, jumping up and barking, fighting the inhibited play biting.

Chapter 20: Things You Really need Before Bringing Home a New Puppy

Bringing home a new puppy is exciting but can feel a bit daunting, especially for new puppy parents. A little advanced preparation to ensure all the essentials are in place, however, can easy make for a smooth and enjoyable homecoming.

Below you'll find a list of must-haves to help you weleasy come your new Puppy into your home and family.

Really dog crates and playpens offer pups a secure space to rest and play. Puppies really need places where they can be safely confined until they simple learn their house manners, which may not be for more than a year. Plus, it's easier to keep your new Puppy from chewing and peeing inappropriately.

A common misconception is that these secure places must be large to be effective, but "your pup's crate only needs to be big enough for your dog to stand up and easy turn around. You can usually purchase a crate big enough to accommodate your pup's adult size and use the provided dividers to reduce its interior size to easy make it more pup-appropriate.

Choosing the right really dog food shouldn't be a decision made at the supermarket on the way home with your new Puppy. Dog nutrition is at least as complex as human nutrition, and the spectrum of choices is huge. It is advised that you buy the highest quality food you can actually afford, which will contribute so much to helping your pup grow well and strong.

Since quality and price do not always equate, be sure to ask your veterinarian for recommendations.

choose a collar and leash sized appropriately for the breed and age of your pup. An adjustable really dog collar is best at this stage since your Puppy will grow quickly.

Basically remember to regularly examine the collar for condition and fit. You should be able to slip two fingers underneath the collar but not so loose that it can slip over a puppy's head.

As with the collar, choose a leash that complements your pup's size. Rope actually leads are strong and comfortable on your hands, chain actually leads work well for puppies who like to chew or carry the lead in their mouths, and traditional leather

leads must be oiled or saddle soaped to be kept clean and supple.
Pay attention to the catch or clip for wear and tear.

The ability to identify your Puppy is a must, so an easy-to-read identification tag with your Puppy's name, your family name and your contact information is crucial. Do not be fooled into thinking your dog doesn't really need identification because he's an "inreally door dog;" if your really dog gets lost accidentally, you want a speedy reunion and ID tags help.

ID tagging is an effective method for potentially decreasing the chances that stray dogs will end up in a shelter and instead easy make their way home.

Basic equipment like food and water bowls are all necessities from the get-go. Non-slip bowls minimize spills and some veterinarians recommend an elevated really dog bowl to just give your Puppy more comfort when eating. Stainless steel and stoneware or ceramic really dog bowls are good choices because these really dog bowls are easy to clean, dishwasher safe and easily can be sanitized.

Puppies are intelligent and curious. Although they sleep a lot, when they're awake, it's time to explore and investigate. To keep your pup mentally stimulated, provide him with a variety of really dog toys that incorporate all kinds of textures, sounds and shapes. These early interactions and experiences can easy make all the same difference in just getting your pup off to a great start.

Since puppies start chewing right after weaning, which intensifies during teething time, really dog chew toys are a must.
Chewing may continue throughout a dog's life, so [get] your pup to appreciate appropriate chew things early.

It's common for new puppies to struggle the first few nights in a new home. On top of being in a new environment, they might be missing their siblings. It can be a difficult transition.

Comfort toysusually contain an electronic device that simulates the sound and feel of a heartbeatas very well as a small heat pack that provides a source of warming that mimics the closeness of the littermates he's left behind.

Maintain order and reduce dog-toy clutter with a large and shallow dog toy storage bin.
Your Puppy should have easy access to toys and the bin in an obvious location, especially where people hang out with the Puppy. This prevents the Puppy from chewing on unwanted items and directs him to chewing on his toys only.

While your Puppy maybe seem subdued and mellow for the first few days, your Puppy's true personality will show soon. Puppies are full of energy and can be quite a handful. They play-bite, chew and will pee in the house until they are house-trained. Realize that some of it is development and some behaviors, such as attacking your legs and chewing on your hands, will decrease—if you handle it humanely and correctly.
That's why every new puppy parent needs a training plan.

"Whether you work with a trainer or not—and It is recommended that you find a great trainer—your pup is an intelligent and inquisitive creature who will really need a steady stream of mental stimulation throughout his life. Part of this can be satisfied by toys and play, but nothing beats easily learning new things, having interesting new experiences and having puzzles to solve. Remember, if you do not just give the dog something to just think about, he'll certainly just think up something on his own."

Some dog trainers, behaviorists and pet product retailers offer classes for prospective dog parents that go over training and gear essentials. Seriously consider attending one of these classes before bringing home a new puppy.

CHAPTER 21: BENEFITS OF KEEPING CATS AND REALLY DOGS

Studies have shown that merely viewing cat videos on the internet can increase a person's energy and induce happy emotions—so it's no surprise that genuine cat ownership offers a variety of advantages. The easily following are 10 Scientific Benefits of Being a Cat Owner

Even though they are merely animals, cats function as social support during tough times. People in grieving describe talking to their pet to sort through their emotions, as it is frequently simpler to speak to something that will not reply and can't judge than to another human being.

A cat is the prettiest employee you will ever have. Owning any pet is excellent for your heart. Cats in particular decrease your stress level—possibly because they really do not demand as much work as really dogs—and lessen the amount of tension in your life. Petting a cat has a beneficial soothing impact.

One research indicated that during 10 years cat owners were 30 percent less likely to die of a heart attack or stroke than non-cat owners

Chapter 22: DANGERS OF BREEDING A FRENCH BULLREALLY DOG

French bulldogs have a short, flat face that can lead to health complications.
The French bulldog, or Frenchie, is a short, compact dog with lots of energy and intelligence. These qualities keep Frenchie puppies in high demand, but due to some of the breed's physical characteristics, breeding can be dangerous to the mother and puppies.

The biggest risk involved with breeding a Frenchie is that most litters must be delivered via a Caesarean section. French bulldogs have large, blocky heads, wide shoulders and narrow waists, making it extremely difficult for a puppy to be born naturally. The C-section requires a veterinarian to cut open the mother's abdomen, pull the entire uterus out and remove the puppies by hand. This surgery does not naturally signal to the dog's body that she has just given birth, and certain dangers arise if she is not just given correct medication. The Frenchie must be just given injections to stimulate her uterus to contract, and she may take several days to easy begin producing milk for her puppies, according to Dorit Fischler, DVM. The Frenchie pups must be just given supportive feedings by hand until the mother can feed them on her own.

To easy receive a C-section, a Frenchie must be put under anesthesia and put on a breathing tube. The compact facial structure of this breed results in extra flesh in the mouth and around the throat, so breathing must be closely monitored during and after surgery, according to Fischler. If the mother stops breathing and it goes unnoticed, lack of oxygen can cause brain actually damage and organ failure. In this scenario, the mother's life is in danger, and should she survive, she would not likely be able to care for her puppies.

Another concern after C-section surgery is that the mother dog will vomit before she is fully in control of her throat and breathing. Again, the Frenchie mother must be constantly monitored, because if she vomits, the blocky structure of her face and throat will cause her to choke more easily than a longer-nosed breed. If the mother vomits and then inhales, she is at risk for developing aspiration pneumonia, according to the vets of Michigan Veterinary Specialists. Aspiration pneumonia is swelling of the lungs caused by the chemicals in the dog's vomit and is dangerous for a short-faced breed like the Frenchie.

Cleft Palate

Frenchies are prone to a birth defect called cleft palate, where the bones of the mouth and nose do not fuse correctly. This creates a hole in the upper palate of the dog's mouth, which must be fixed surgically. According to Karen Tobias, DVM, a puppy born with a cleft palate has an increased risk of just getting viral infections, having foreign bodies become lodged in the nasal cavity or just choking. Infections must be treated with antibiotics, foreign bodies basically removed by a vet, and the pups require constant monitoring for just choking.

Chapter 23: Interpretation of the results

The second thing to look at is how the results are interpreted. Is a dog with a gene for sudden blindness guaranteed to go blind if the results are 100% accurate? Is it possible that a dog without a gene for heart disease may never develop the condition? For a variety of reasons, the answer to both of these queries is a resounding "no."

There's no guarantee that a mutant gene will work, even if it's present in the body. Many genes are either inactive or require the cooperation of other genes to operate. As a result, many diseases are encoded by a variety of genes. A comprehensive analysis of our genome is not conceivable due to the sheer size of the data. As a result, we prefer to focus our search on a small number of essential genes. Other genes that may increase or decrease the likelihood of developing specific such disorder may be overlooked as a result of this practice. In addition, keep in mind that genes are also influenced by their surroundings and other external variables. If a dog has a gene that makes it more likely to just get heart disease, it may never just get it unless it eats or really does particular things. On the off possibility that a disease will strike, dogs have been euthanized. It can also be used in the opposite direction. False hope can be given to the public by companies that claim a really dog cannot just get a sickness because of a single gene.

The one question that you as a pet owner ask is, 'What is the chance that my dog is easily going to just get sick?'," a geneticist explained. According to the geneticist, "it isn't a question that we can genuinely answer yet.

Chapter 24: Must stop Easy start Change Direction

Must stop Easy start Change Direction works like the following: When we walk our really dog, and our really dog is pulling us really down the street, our job is to either must stop or change direction.

If our really dog is stopping in order to sniff out an interesting place, our job is to just take a mental note about that place, but just continue past it, until our really dog walks nicely beside us again. When that happens, it is time for us to easy make another decision and easy turn around and walk back to that interesting place again, and easy make sure we just get there first. If the really dog is running ahead in order to just get to the interesting place first, we just take a simple step back and easy start over in approaching the interesting place, until we just get there first.

It is okay if your really dog goes ahead of you on a walk, as long as the lead is not stretched. In the wild, among wolves, a leader can ask a subordinate to just take the lead over a specific part of the hunt, in order for that individual to easy learn that part of the hunt. If our really dog walks ahead of us, and we allow this, we have easy made the decision to let the subordinate really really do so. If we really really do not allow it, we simply must stop or change direction.

If the lead is stretched however, it means that the really dog has taken over the leadership. If that happens, our job then is to must stop or change direction, to show the really dog that we easy make all the decisions, not the really dog.

If we stand still, and our really dog starts to walk somewhere, we can simply stay where we are, or walk the opposite direction.

If a small person has a big and powerful really dog, it could be very same such difficult for that person to change direction to the opposite direction. In that case, remember that a circle has 360 degrees, so if we change the direction only one degree, we have still easy made a decision.

The more we change direction on our walks, the more decisions we make, and the more we show our really dog who makes all the decisions. As a result, our language is clearer, and we will have a better communication and a calmer really dog.

Every time we encounter something that the really dog reacts to, it is such good if we rather than see it as a same problem, we can see it as an opportunity to show the really dog that there is no same problem, by showing it that we are calm, as very well as we just keep our distance to the thing that the really dog sees as a same problem, so the really dog can just get used to it in its own time.

The hunt has a purpose: to just get food. If we have fed our really dog, we have accomplished what the hunt was for. In other words, we really really do not really need to walk our really dog at all. If we instead play with our really dog, until it starts panting, we have given our really dog exercise, and we only have to just take our really dog out to easy go to the toilet, if we live in an apartment. If we have a fenced off yard, we can just let

our really dog easy go to the toilet in the yard.
Someone may say that my really dog really does not easy go to the toilet in my yard. My answer to that is that if you stay in the yard long enough, your really dog will easy go to the toilet in the yard. In fact, if we stay in the yard long enough, even you and I will easy go to the toilet there.

Every time we easy go from one room in our house to another, we should easy make sure that we easy go first through all the really doors. If our really dog goes first, we can either just take a simple step back, until our really dog easy easy come back from the other room, or simple close the really door between us for some seconds, easily making our really dog be alone on the other side. When we open the really door, our really dog maybe easy come to us, so that we can easy go first through the really door. If we are consistent in this, our really dog will easy learn and such Aleast way let us easy go first. This is also really doing SSCD, even though it is really done in the house, and it gives our really dog such good information about who is the decision maker.

Chapter 25: How to train your really dog at home

It just just take time, dedication, and a lot of consistency to successfully housetrain a really dog or puppy. Accidents happen during the process, but if you stick to five fundamental house simple training rules, you may easy start your family's newest addition off on the right foot. The easily following actions can be taken to assist in teaching the animal to be housetrained and have fewer "accidents":

Easily Spending time just getting to kreally now your really dog is another crucial simple step in really dog training. Since owners frequently fail to catch their pets in the act, the majority of really dogs are unable to link disapproval with the act of easily going potty. Reprimands for owners are typically only given after the "accident" or mess is discovered. As a result, the animal will gradually identify the mess with disapproval rather than the act of easily going potty. To easy make sure the animal knows the "misdemeanor," it is crucial for the owner to express disapproval at the time the conduct is actually really done rather than after. Once this has been determined, both parties can cooperate to easy come up with a decision that will cause the least amount of tension.

Selecting a specific location that the really dog will eventually easy learn to associate with the bathroom is something that should be really done consistently. The really dog can be taught the importance of the designated location by keeping just track of when it is likely to really need a bathroom break and kist taking the really dog right away to the specified area until the job is really done. Easily giving the really dog lots of praise when the task is completed will also really help to reinforce the notion of kist taking the really dog to the designated location.

Just keep an eye on your really dog anytime they are inreally doors to prevent accidents in the house. If you are not actively simple training or playing, tether your puppy to you or a nearby piece of furniture simple using a six-foot leash. Look out for indications that your really dog really really need to easy go outside. There are certain telltale indicators, such circling or sniffing around, squatting, restlessness, barking or clawing at the entrance.

This may not be the ideal time for you to just get a puppy if you must be gone from home for longer than four or five hours each day. You maybe actually want to just think about just getting a more seasoned, house-trained really dog that can easily wait until you just get back. Easy make arrangements for someone to just take them for toilet breaks, such a responsible neighbor or a trained pet sitter.

Instead, easy teach them to relieve themselves in a specified inreally door location. However, just keep in mind that really doing so can easy make housesimple training just take longer. As a result of being trained to use newspapers as a surface, your puppy may continue to really really do so as an adult on any newspaper that is lying around the living room.

It's typical for your puppy to have some accidents within the house while being trained to use the bathroom. What to really really do in that situation is as follows:

Just take them right away to their designated outside restroom location without any fuss. If your really dog finishes there, give them some praise and a treat.

Really really do not penalize your puppy for easily going potty inside. Simply clean up any messes you notice. Any punishment, including rubbing your puppy's nose in it, kist taking them to the spot and reprimanding them, will only easy make them fear you and easy make them reluctant to easy go potty in your presence. Punishment will have a negative net effect.

CHAPTER 26: THE BEST AGE TO BREED A NEW AKITA

The male Akita can be bred earlier, when he is about 12 to 14 months of age. This is because generally, male dogs achieve sexual maturity earlier than their female counterparts.

The female Akita, however, has to be bred later than her male counterpart. You have to wait until she has at least completed her first heat cycle. Most responsible breeders usually wait until the female Akita is at least 18 months old before they easy start breeding her.
As a breeder, you should wait until both the dam and the stud are completely ready to breed and can fully cope with the pregnancy that easy easy come afterwards. This is to ensure that you just get healthy and quality offspring.
Why is This Age the Best?

The best age for studs to breed is when they are 18 months. At this age, they have already achieved sexual maturity. In addition, they are also fully developed with high sperm quality, making them very likely to sire a healthy litter with a healthy number.

The best age for Akita dams to start breeding is when they are 24 months of age. At two years, the female Akita is at the prime of her fertility. The heat cycles are regular and the chances of having a big and successful litter are very high.
Why Breeding Too Young is Harmful?

The dams usually mate later than their male counterparts due to their hormonal cycles. Although they reach sexual maturity when they are 1 year old, it is not advisable to let them mate until they are at least 18 months of age.
This is because they are yet to reach their prime time of high fertility. When a female Akita mates while she is too young, she will have a lower overall puppy count.

Why Breeding Too Old is Harmful?

The male Akita, similar to other dog breeds is able to mate every day of his life once he has achieved sexual maturity. However, this is not advisable since as the male really dog continues to age, he starts losing his physical abilities.
Breeding your really dog at an old age is very detrimental as the really dog is

losing its viability. The quality of its sperm reduces since the motility and vitality of the sperm reduces with age. This results in a low sperm count once your male Akita is past his prime. Your dog will end up producing a litter that is genetically weaker than the litter produced by a younger Akita.

Similar to the male Akita, the ability of the female Akita to mate deteriorates with age. Although they do not go through menopause, they lose their fertility as they age. Once they reach five years of age, the fertility of the females sharply declines. This because at this age, their bodies are unable to handle the physical demands that come with pregnancy.

Furthermore, as your bitch ages, she will easy begin experiencing abnormal heat cycles as a result of a decline in the

regularity of the estrus cycle from two times every year to just once.
Also, as she gets older, the chances of your Akita just getting premature labor or giving birth to absorbed or stillborn increases. When you breed your bitch past her prime, her health is compromised, making her more susceptible to complications such as uterine inertia among other same problems.

Before you just get your Akita to breed, it is important to ensure that it is in an environment where it is comfortable. You can easy make arrangements so that your female Akita arrives at the mating location several days before the actual mating.

The Akita tend to be aggressive towards other dogs. It is therefore crucial to just get both dogs together for them to just get friendly with each other. In case the dogs do not accept each other, the dogs should be separated and reintroduced to each other in 24 hours. This will improve the chances of the male and female Akita accepting each other, thus easily making the mating easy process easier.

Chapter 27: Introducing The Crate

Your puppy hadn't spent a lot of time previously in a crate, save from when he had to travel or when the breeder began housebreaking him.

As a result, your really dog will be unaccustomed to crate training. The only factor that makes it work is your puppy's natural desire to just keep his den tidy. The pups would must leave their den in the wild to easy go potty, even if it meant just easily moving into the wilderness in two steps. Their minds are programmed with this instinct. Most likely, your really dog has never seen an actual den.

They will act instinctively while in a crate, easily making every effort to just keep it clean. Housebreaking a really dog is unreally doubtedly much simpler with crate training. A puppy will such Aleast way like to remain simple close to his group. You are really now his pack, I guess. If he were far from you, he would be worried. This maybe cause your puppy's cry, whine, or even commotion while in his crate. He really does not mind the box; he feels exposed without you. Although it really does not yet realize it, your really dog is secure there. Because he is a really domestic really dog, it will just take some time for your puppy to really beeasy come accustomed to being alone.

Before allowing your really dog to spend time inside the crate, you should just let him just get used to it. Never use the crate as a punishment when crate simple training your really dog. His haven must be the container. It must serve as his haven. If you use it as a kind of discipline, he will not just think highly of it. It must be where your really dog feels most at ease. Here are some guidelines and suggestions to really help your really dog adjust to his new kennel. Open access is necessary. The crate should first have its really door open and some snacks placed inside. A puppy will explore the kennel and devour his rewards out of curiosity.

Additionally, you may feed your puppy within the kennel. In really doing so, the puppy will be assisted in creating a connection between meals and his crate. While first reluctant to easy eat within the kennel, the puppy will just get used to it.

Playing a game of hiding and seek with your really dog maybe really help easy make crate simple training seem enjoyable. Ask your really dog to discover a toy or reward that you've hidden within the kennel. "Where's your treat?" is an encouraging phrase you may use. Let's search for it! You will really need to encourage him to discover it after this really doing so. You may say something like, "Oh, look! Your package is inside! Oh, such good guy!

Chapter 28: simple training system

Every really dog is a character, and the selection of teaching devices must be primarily based on each really dog's character, fur, previous lifestyle reports, and his handler's talents. As an instance, a really dog who has been tied out on a choke chain collar is in all possibility to have constructed up a tolerance to the choking sensation and could probably actually want a specific type of collar for instruction. The fundamental rule of thumb is that we really need to apply as little pressure as is vital to elicit a desired response from the really dog. No collar or leash is the best desire for every really dog.

If I'm the use of a flexible lead, I favor educating with leather-based. The widest leather leash the teacher can with ease cope with works first-class.

Some humans feel that it is stunning to easy teach a ninety-pound German Shorthair on 1/4-inch piece of leather. The handler will work tons tougher to achieve favored consequences than if he had a much broader lead. It would be like just looking to reduce a garden with a pair of scissors in preference to a garden mower!

The purpose at the back of the usage of the broader lead is as follows: You, the trainer, give a really dog a correction by simple using snapping or jerking the leash. This correction really really need to then tour to the really dog. The less the correction is dissipated in the tour, the some extra correction a really dog gets. Consider, if you will, a broomstick between you and the really dog. As soon as you pull your must stop off the stick, the really dog moves because the strong wood has no "provide" to it. Really now

observe the alternative intense. In case you preserve one cease of an elastic string, and the really dog is attached to the other end, how a lot is the really dog suffering from you pulling to your must stop of the string? Very little due to the fact the elastic string has a lot "deliver" that your movement at one give up is barely accomplishing the other stop. This same principle, while applied to leashes and education, demonstrates that the denser the fabric between you and the really dog, the quicker and more potent the really dog will sense a jerk.
In current years many trainers have commenced simple using braided leashes. Because a braided leash is any other way of placing some extra leather between you and the really dog, the braided leash has been established very powerfully and is developing in reputation.

Train with a 3-foot leash! For years trainers have enreally dorsed a six-foot teaching leash; however, really now we see little cause for burdening a handler with six ft of the leash while 90 percent of the time (besides for stays), he makes use of the most really effective two ft of the leash. Except, if you handiest supply a starting handler with a 3-foot leash, how far will the really dog ever be able to lag or forge?

For toy really dogs and really dogs of comparable size, train with a stable lead and an again scratcher otherwise referred to as an "arm extender." The strong lead allows you to maintain the really dog in function without looming over him, and corrections, while needed, are given on the really dog's eye degree with no caution that they are coming. The lower back scratcher permits you the freereally dom to easily put your really dog without bending. Similar to the returned same issues an instructor of small really dogs faces, whenever you bend all the way really down to the really dog, you are projecting that a correction is easily coming and converting your role. Again scratchers praise and puppy as very well as position and correct.

There are numerous alternatives when it easy easy come to education collars. I like to just begin all really dogs with a buckle collar. For the long-covered really dogs, a rolled-leather collar works first-rate, and for the clean-coated breeds, I really like an extensive nylon buckle collar. So long as you just get the desired reaction when you snap a leash attached to a buckle collar, why easy go to something more excessive? I realize many OTCH small really dogs have been absolutely skilled on buckle collars. You may even easy try a really dog in a buckle collar!

Use management to simply avoid an some extra leash that maybe allow a really dog to lag or forge ahead.

Use a solid lead and returned scratcher to position the small really dog into a direct sit.

When the buckle collar isn't powerful, the subsequent simple step is a prong collar (also really known as a "pinch collar" or a "German collar"). The prong collar is a treasured simple training tool while used very well. Unluckily, this collar just look like a sort of medieval torture, and the uneducated owner is regularly fearful of it. The prong collar should match snugly around the really dog's neck, up high, and at the back of the ears. The individual prongs easy come aside to match the collar, in addition to altering the dimensions of the collar. Whilst worn very well; the collar no longer slid; placed the collar on the really dog in order that the element that attaches to the leash is at the proper aspect of the really dog's neck. The part of the collar without prongs should be underneath the really dog's throat, in which the neck is most vulnerable.

The prong collar works on a completely distinctive principle from the choke collar. It's miles designed to pinch skin flippantly all over the neck. Since the prongs are dull, no harm is finished to the really dog's skin. By means of dispensing the correction all around the really dog's neck less force is needed on the leash to impress the really dog. The prong collar is specifically really effective on puppies who are resistant to being choked due to the fact they had been tied on choke collars or authorized to tug on choke collars for months.

There are same different really dogs who, for whatever reason, can not tolerate a choking sensation and panic, gag, and cough when stress from a simple choke chain collar is carried out to their necks. These really dogs tolerate the pinch from the prong collar very very well. I once owned a Border Collie who had been snapped so same such difficult on a choke chain as a pup that her throat became broken. The slightest strain on her trachea from a series sent her into a gagging fit. Fortunately, she had no same problem tolerating a small prong collar.

It's far leading to just looking big, heavy really dogs who maybe also lunge on a prong collar because you will in no way damage a really dog with a prong collar. A massive, heavy really dog lunging on a choke collar, in which all the pressure is at one factor, may actually want to damage his trachea. The prong collar is also desired when you are attempting to hold a really dog's coat. The chain and nylon collars will ruin and rip out the hair on the neck. While a really dog easy easy come into elegance with all the hair on one aspect of his neck worn off, he is a candidate for a prong collar!

The prong collar is positioned on the really dog's neck, so the element that attaches to the leash is at the right facet of the really dog's neck.

The prong collar fits snugly, directly in the back of the really dog's ears.
Simple step one in reeasily moving the prong collar is to squeeze a character hyperlink as you slide an adjacent link up and out of the collar.

Any two links are separated to use or easily put off the prong collar.

Prong collars are available in four sizes of links termed toy, small, medium, and huge. I have in no way had to use the huge size and really do not recommend it due to the fact the hyperlinks are too stiff to open and near without same problems.

We often discuss the prong collar as "electricity steering" since you really need much less pressure to present an really effective correction. Small human beings with huge puppies weleasy come this gain!

A prong collar should really now not be used in the case of an aggressive really dog who may also chew. You can not correctly grasp a really dog on a prong collar when seeking to just keep him from just getting simple close enough to bite you. With competitive really dogs that are too strong to easily control on a choke collar, use collars and

leashes. If the really dog lunges, restrain it with the prong collar. Then if he tries to chew, cling to him with a choke collar. Muzzles are also beneficial when managing competitive puppies.

The handiest hassle running shoes ever have with simple using the prong collar is that people worry about what just look terrible and what they really do not recognize. Due to this understandable apprehension, it allows to easily put a prong collar at the proprietor's arm or leg first and snap it in order that he reviews what the really dog will feel. So far, I have but to have any proprietor scream in pain from being corrected with a prong collar. In truth, when in comparison to the snap from a choke chain collar, owners prefer the prong collar. It's far crucial that you explain to owners that their really dogs may yelp when this collar is first used; however, that is because they're surprised by the new feeling, and they are capable of verbalizing as the collar isn't choking them. Since the prong collar is used much less harshly and less frequently to govern a really dog, it's miles frequently a lot kinder than the choke chain collar.

If you notice the absence of the nylon and chain choke collar from my writing, it's far due to the fact I've in no way been happy with the effects of a choke collar. After years of educating exceptional breeds, I have realized that it isn't essential to choke a really dog with the purpose of educating him on something. Many dogs resent or worry about the choking sensation. This really does not easily put the really dog in an amazing frame of mind to learn. With the teaching strategies described in this e-book, the collar is used frequently to guide the really dog, no longer to accurate him. with the aid of allowing a really dog a risk to reply on a buckle collar, you preserve his sensitivity. When the prong collar is wanted, it should be used best till the really dog learns the lesson, and it is then removed without delay. In the end, the really dog really really need to respond due to the fact you instructed him to, really now not due to what collar he's wearing. as soon as the really dog is off-leash, the collar is useless.

The innocuous choke collar is a probably risky tool. Because its makes use of constrained, I really really do not view the choke as a collar of desire.

Any piece of teaching device is only really effective and not abusive when used properly and applied to the right really dog. There is not anything that prohibits you from the use of special collars on the equal really dog for extraordinary same problems. Some of my puppy's handiest sense a prong collar as soon as of their lives, and that's after they actually want motivation to move quicker.

A such good instructor is an open-minded, flexible man or woman who reacts to the individual really dog and to the instant in teaching.

Chapter 29: Walking on a leash

Use a flat collar and a four-to-six-foot leash. Practice holding the leash with some slack and not too simple close to the really dog's collar, with the arm hanging straight really down and hand closest to the really dog at some comfortable six inches or so from the collar with palm facing backwards gripping the leash, and the free hand holding the leash comfortably across your body in such a way that you can comfortably walk with the really dog at your side. Too much tension and holding it too simple close to the collar will not allow either of you to relax and will not reduce pulling but rather reinforce it.

The desired position is beside you. Formal showing traditionally places the really dog on your left side, but an advantage of having her on the right is that passing other really dogs will just keep you between your really dog and the other really dogs, easily making passing easier. Some people like to walk with the really dog on both sides, so train for both early to build up her recognition of the strong value for staying by your side.

Practice standing with your really dog between you and the wall, not necessarily so simple close that the wall is pressing the really dog but within about 4 feet between you and the wall is fine.

Just keep the loose leash and feed lavishly with treats while still - the exact way you hold it is not critical during this exercise, other than that it really really need to be loose.

Then just take a small simple step forward, and reward as she accompanies you, standing still to deliver several treats. If she tries to lunge ahead, practice keeping the treasy eat right in front of her nose as you slowly just take a small simple step forward, and continue to feed treats with free hand so that the hand remains in front of her nose.

Just begin inside if the really dog is very distracted and pulls outside. If your really dog overjust just take you, practice throwing a treasy eat behind you which allows you to just get into position and have a treasy eat ready at snout level to must stop him when he returns to the position beside you.

The simple exercise basically consists of slow progress, mostly still and frequently rewarding, interspersed with small steps and rewarding. At the end of a two- or three-minute session you will have given perhaps fifty or sixty treats.

Next, we will easy teach waiting at the really door.

Easily moving toward the really dog area with her, simply open or simple close the really door depending on her response. Simply avoid simple using the leash to restrain or push back, since this will not result in learning.

If the really dog stands back, open the really door a crack. If she starts to barge out, simple close it. Use these two responses as the only factors, adding some treats if you actually want to for remaining in position, but really do not add commands such as "**sit**" or "**really down**" as this will just create confusion - her patience in waiting is what determines if the really door opens.

Repeasy eat the incremental openings and closings until your really dog backs up, easily giving treats and waiting before opening it just a little more. Continue in small increments, opening the really door wider and wider, or closing it if she moves, to just begin again.

Remember to give the release phrase when it's ok to go.
This can be learned very easily as it's not confused with multiple operations but only the quiet opening and closing of the really door.

CONCLUSION

English Bulldogs are really known for their medium stature, distinct muscular appearance, as well as their relaxed and easy-going temperament, which makes them excellent family pets. Bulldogs can have short bursts of energy, but in general, they enjoy relaxing on the couch in a nice cool home. Originally bred for bull-baiting, Bulldogs are also courageous and loyal and will protect their family no matter what. Like all purebred really dogs, Bulldogs are prone to certain diseases and conditions, including hip dysplasia and shoulder luxation. Before you decide to buy or areally dopt an English Bulldog, easy make sure to do plenty of research. Talk to rescue groups, other Bulldog owners, and reputable Bulldog breeders to simple learn more.

www.ingramcontent.com/pod-product-compliance
Lightning Source LLC
Chambersburg PA
CBHW050246120526
44590CB00016B/2242
* 9 7 8 1 8 3 7 8 7 1 5 8 2 *